MOUNTAIN LION VS. COYOTE

BY THOMAS K. ADAMSON

BELLWETHER MEDIA • MINNEAPOLIS, MN

Torque brims with excitement
perfect for thrill-seekers of all kinds.
Discover daring survival skills, explore
uncharted worlds, and marvel at mighty
engines and extreme sports. In *Torque* books,
anything can happen. Are you ready?

This edition first published in 2021 by Bellwether Media, Inc.

No part of this publication may be reproduced in whole or in part without written
permission of the publisher. For information regarding permission, write to
Bellwether Media, Inc., Attention: Permissions Department,
6012 Blue Circle Drive, Minnetonka, MN 55343.

Library of Congress Cataloging-in-Publication Data

Names: Adamson, Thomas K., 1970- author.
Title: Mountain lion vs. coyote / Thomas K. Adamson.
Other titles: Mountain lion versus coyote
Description: Minneapolis, MN : Bellwether Media, 2021. | Series: Torque:
    animal battles | Includes bibliographical references and index. |
    Audience: Ages 7-12 | Audience: Grades 4-6 | Summary: "Amazing
    photography accompanies engaging information about the fighting
    abilities of mountain lions and coyotes. The combination of
    high-interest subject matter and light text is intended for students in
    grades 3 through 7"– Provided by publisher.
Identifiers: LCCN 2020041134 (print) | LCCN 2020041135 (ebook) | ISBN
    9781644874615 (library binding) | ISBN 9781648342547 (paperback) | ISBN
    9781648341380 (ebook)
Subjects: LCSH: Puma–Juvenile literature. | Coyote–Juvenile literature.
Classification: LCC QL737.C23 A23 2021 (print) | LCC QL737.C23 (ebook) |
    DDC 599.75/24–dc23
LC record available at https://lccn.loc.gov/2020041134
LC ebook record available at https://lccn.loc.gov/2020041135

Editor: Kieran Downs   Designer: Josh Brink

Printed in the United States of America, North Mankato, MN.

TABLE OF CONTENTS

THE COMPETITORS

Two sneaky **predators** roam North America. Mountain lions are silent hunters. Their surprise leaps make it hard for **prey** to escape.

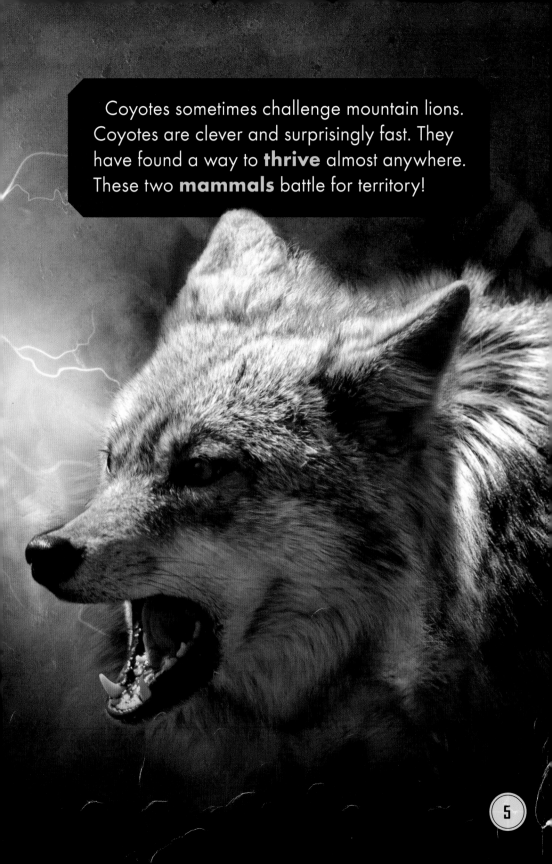

Coyotes sometimes challenge mountain lions. Coyotes are clever and surprisingly fast. They have found a way to **thrive** almost anywhere. These two **mammals** battle for territory!

MOUNTAIN LION PROFILE

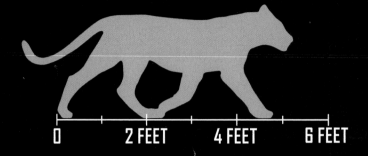

```
0          2 FEET      4 FEET      6 FEET
```

BODY LENGTH
UP TO 5 FEET
(1.5 METERS)

WEIGHT
UP TO 158 POUNDS
(72 KILOGRAMS)

HABITAT

SWAMPS

DESERTS

MOUNTAINS

FORESTS

MOUNTAIN LION RANGE

■ RANGE

At up to 5 feet (1.5 meters) long, mountain lions are large members of the cat family. They live in many **habitats** across North and South America. They make their homes in forests, mountains, swamps, and even deserts.

These cats mainly hunt deer. They will also eat smaller animals such as rabbits or squirrels.

MOUNTAIN LION NAMES

Mountain lions go by many other names. They are also called cougars, pumas, panthers, and catamounts.

Coyotes live in most of North America and Central America. These lean predators have grayish brown fur and round, bushy tails.

Coyotes have a good sense of smell. Even though they are mostly found on the **plains**, these wild dogs will go wherever there is food. That can even mean living in cities.

OUT FOR A SWIM

Coyotes are great swimmers. This has allowed them to live on islands!

COYOTE PROFILE

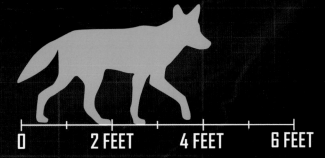

0   2 FEET   4 FEET   6 FEET

LENGTH
UP TO 4.3 FEET
(1.3 METERS)

WEIGHT
UP TO 50 POUNDS
(23 KILOGRAMS)

HABITAT

PLAINS   FORESTS   DESERTS   CITIES

COYOTE RANGE

RANGE

SECRET WEAPONS

Both predators sneak up on prey. Mountain lions do most of their hunting at night. Their excellent eyesight allows them to spot prey in the dark. This lets them attack their prey unseen.

COYOTE

SHARP SENSE OF SMELL

SPEED

STAMINA

Coyotes **stalk** prey silently. They use their strong sense of smell. They can **track** prey as it moves through thick trees and brush.

SECRET WEAPONS

EXCELLENT EYESIGHT

SHARP, RETRACTABLE CLAWS

STRONG BACK LEGS

Mountain lions have sharp, curved claws on their large front paws. The claws are **retractable**. They stay protected and sharp until they are needed.

Coyotes chase after prey with super speeds. They are one of the fastest animals in North America. They can run at speeds of more than 40 miles (64 kilometers) per hour!

COYOTE TOP SPEED

40 MPH (64 KM/H)

28 MPH (45 KM/H)

MORE THAN 40 MILES (64 KILOMETERS) PER HOUR

COYOTE

28 MILES (45 KILOMETERS) PER HOUR

HUMAN

MOUNTAIN LION LEAPING DISTANCE

MOUNTAIN LION
40 FEET (12 METERS)

| 0 FEET | 10 FEET | 20 FEET | 30 FEET | 40 FEET |

LONG JUMP WORLD RECORD
29.36 FEET (8.95 METERS)

| 0 FEET | 10 FEET | 20 FEET | 30 FEET | 40 FEET |

Mountain lions have powerful back legs. They can jump as far as 40 feet (12 meters) in one leap. They use this power to pounce on prey.

Coyotes wear down prey with their great **stamina**. They can chase large prey like deer for long distances. They attack when the animal is tired.

ATTACK MOVES

Mountain lions hide and wait for a good time to attack. They leap forward when they are close enough. Sharp claws dig into the neck and shoulders of their prey.

Coyotes attack differently depending on their prey. They pounce on small prey. They use their teeth to wound the animal.

NO SCARY ROAR

Mountain lions cannot roar.
They growl, hiss, and purr,
just like house cats!

A sudden attack from a mountain lion can knock prey off balance. The cats attack the back of the neck with their powerful jaws. One bite usually takes down prey.

Coyotes wear down large prey. Pairs may take turns chasing prey. Then the coyotes bite at their prey's back legs. They finish them with a bite to the throat.

READY, FIGHT!

A hungry mountain lion spots a coyote in its territory. It sneaks closer. The coyote smells something. It senses danger.

The mountain lion pounces, claws out. The coyote sprints forward, teeth bared. The coyote tries to bite the mountain lion. But the lion is quicker. It grabs the coyote and bites its neck. This fight is over!

GLOSSARY

habitats—the homes or areas where animals prefer to live

mammals—warm-blooded animals that have backbones and feed their young milk

plains—large areas of flat land

predators—animals that hunt other animals for food

prey—animals that are hunted by other animals for food

retractable—able to be pulled back in

stalk—to follow closely and quietly

stamina—the energy and strength to keep doing something without becoming tired

thrive—to live well

track—to look for prey by following marks left behind, like scents

TO LEARN MORE

AT THE LIBRARY

Gagne, Tammy. *Coyotes*. Lake Elmo, Minn.: Focus Readers, 2017.

Hogan, Christa C. *Mountain Lions*. Lake Elmo, Minn.: North Star Editions, 2017.

Sommer, Nathan. *Lion vs. Hyena Clan*. Minneapolis, Minn.: Bellwether Media, 2020.

ON THE WEB

FACTSURFER

Factsurfer.com gives you a safe, fun way to find more information.

1. Go to www.factsurfer.com

2. Enter "mountain lion vs. coyote" into the search box and click Q.

3. Select your book cover to see a list of related content.

INDEX

The images in this book are reproduced through the courtesy of: Debbie Steinhausser, cover (mountain lion); Robi George / Getty Images, cover (coyote); Reimar, pp. 4, 5; Geoffrey Kuchera, pp. 6-7; Doug Oglesby, pp. 8-9; Kwadrat, p. 10; Matt Knoth, p. 11; Osaze Cuomo, p. 11 (speed); Harry Collins Photography, p. 11 (sharp sense of smell); Warren Metcalf, p. 11 (stamina); Dennis W Donohue, p. 12; TigerStocks, p. 12 (excellent eyesight); Mikhail Kolesnikov, p. 12 (sharp, retractable claws); Václav Sebek, p. 12 (strong back legs); GarysFRP, p. 13; Tony Rix, p. 14; Dominique Braud/Dembinsky Photo Associates / Alamy Stock Photo, p. 15; agefotostock / Alamy Stock Photo, p. 16; jhayes44, p. 17; Robert Pickett / Alamy Stock Photo, p. 18; Robert McGouey/Wildlife / Alamy Stock Photo, p. 19; Sarah Cheriton-Jones, pp. 20-21 (mountain lion); Melanie DeFazio, pp. 20-21 (mountain lion); Jan Havlicek, pp. 20-21 (coyote).